# Animal Eggs

An Amazing Clutch of Mysteries & Marvels!

# Animal Eggs

An Amazing Clutch of Mysteries & Marvels!

Dawn Cusick & Joanne O'Sullivan

EarlyLight Books

Waynesville, North Carolina, USA

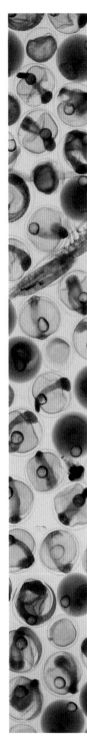

— To the katydid *Amblycorypha alexanderi,* whose egg-laying behavior inspired a fascination with animal eggs
— DC

— For my hatchlings, Maeve and Finn . . .
— JO

**Cover Design:** Stewart Pack
**Page Design:** Stewart Pack
**Photo Research:** Beth Fielding
**Copy Editors:** Susan Brill, Catherine Ham

10 9 8 7 6 5 4 3 2 1

First edition

Published by EarlyLight Books, Inc.

1436 Dellwood Road, Waynesville, NC  28786, USA

© 2011 EarlyLight Books, Inc.

Manufactured in China.

ISBN-13: 978-0-9797455-3-9

ISBN-10: 0-9797455-3-5

**Cataloging Information**
Cusick, Dawn.
　　　Animal eggs/Dawn Cusick
　　　　　48  p. : col. ill. ; 20 cm.
　　　Includes index (p.).
　　　Summary: Explores the morphology and behavior of egg-laying animals and
　　　　　their eggs.  Includes a range of taxa, including mammals, birds
　　　　　　insects, spiders, reptiles, fish, cephalopods, coral, parasites,
　　　　　and dinosaurs.

　　　LC QL956.5
　　　591.468 dcc
　　　ISBN-13: 978-0-9797455-1-5 (alk. paper)
　　　ISBN-10: 0-9797455-1-9 (alk. paper)
　　　　　Embryology -- juvenile literature
　　　　　Eggs -- juvenile literature

**IMAGE CREDITS:** R. Scott Cameron, Advanced Forest Protection, Inc., Bugwood.org, front cover and 18; Frank Peairs, Colorado State University, Bugwood.org, 13 – top; John Lewis, Deep Sea Images, 13; John H. Ghent, USDA Forest Service, Bugwood.org, 15 – top right; Gyorgy Csoka, Hungary Forest Research Institute, Bugwood.org, 15 – bottom right; Matt Wilson/Jay Clark, NOAA NMFS AFSC, 17; W. M. Ciesla, Forest Health Management International, Bugwood.org, 19 – bottom left; Matt Wilson/Jay Clark, NOAA NMFS AFSC, 21 – top; James Solomon, USDA Forest Service, Bugwood.org, 27 – top left; Susan Ellis, Bugwood.org, 27 – top right; Jack Dykinga/USDA, 30; Whitney Cranshaw, Colorado State University, Bugwood.org, 31 – top right; E. Bradford Walker, Vermont Department of Forests, Parks and Recreation, Bugwood.org, 31 – top left; CDC, 41 – bottom; Alex Pauvolid-Corrêa, Fundação Oswaldo Cruz, Bugwood.org, 41 – bottom right; Lori Oberhofer, National Park Service, Bugwood.org, 41 – top; images courtesy of J. M. Ehrman, Digital Microscopy Facility, Mount Allison University (www.mta.ca/dmf), 40 – bottom left and right; CDC/Harvard University, Dr. Gary Alpert, Dr. Harold Harlan, Richard Pollack, 43 – center top; Gary Alpert, Harvard University, Bugwood.org, 43 – top; CDC, 45 – top left; Lacy L. Hyche, Auburn University, Bugwood.org, 45 – bottom left; Emma Hickerson, 45 and 47 – top right; the University Museum of Zoology, Cambridge, 45 and 47 – bottom right, reproduced with kind permission.

b19577928

# Contents

# Egg Layers

If someone offered you a great prize for every egg-laying animal you could name in five minutes, how many animals could you think of? In the pages that follow, you will meet more than a hundred animals that lay eggs. The animals growing inside these eggs are called embryos, and the yellow food source for the animal is called the yolk sac.

## Hello, Brother!

These five-lined skinks broke through their shells just seconds before this photo was taken.

Reptiles lay eggs with a rubbery, leather-like shell and use a special egg tooth to help cut through the shell when they are ready to emerge.

## Here today, spawn tomorrow

Frogs, toads, and some other amphibians such as salamanders lay eggs in large groups called spawn. Their eggs have a thick jelly coat around them, unlike the hard, outer shell that many other types of animal eggs have.

Male fish often stay with the eggs and "fan" them with their fins. Fanning keeps dirt and parasites away from the eggs, and also brings extra oxygen near them. This clown fish is guarding his orange eggs.

An Egg's Biggest Fan

# Egg Layers

Everyone knows that birds lay eggs in tree nests, but did you know that some birds lay their eggs in ground or water nests?  Even more suprising, two types of mammals also lay eggs.  Most mammals that you know about — cats, dogs, cows, horses — do not lay eggs, but the playtpus and the spiny anteater lay eggs in ground nests.

## Can You Find This Bird's Eggs?

The comb-crested jacana bird from Australia lays its eggs on water plants.  The eggs blend in so well they can be hard to find.  How long did it take you to see them?  The males guard the eggs from snakes and other animals that eat bird eggs.

## Platypus

The platypus lives in burrows that it digs along banks of streams and rivers in Eastern Australia. The female platypus lays her eggs in these burrows. Like other mammals and the spiny anteaters, the platypus can feed her newly hatched offspring with milk made by her body. Egg-laying mammals are called monotremes.

## Spiny Anteaters

There are several species (types) of spiny anteaters that lay eggs. They live in Australia, Tasmania, and New Guinea.

# Egg Layers

Fish are not the only underwater animals that lay eggs. Octopus, squid, lobster, and shrimp also lay eggs. Land animals such as spiders and insects lay eggs, too. Some animals lay hundreds or thousands of eggs at a time, while others lay just a few.

## Sea Eggs

A female octopus lays her eggs in large groups and stays with them until they hatch.

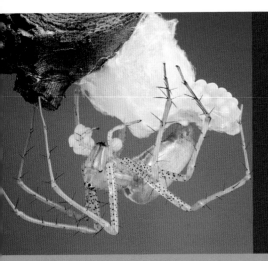

## Lynx spiders

Many spiders spin silk around clusters of their eggs, then the females guard the silken pouch.  This lynx spider will attack any ants that try to eat her eggs. She will also protect her newborn spiderlings for a few weeks after they hatch.

## Break an Egg!

Many insects attach their eggs to plants in large groups.  The insects break out of their eggs when their bodies become too large for the egg's shell.

# Egg Shapes & Sizes

Not all eggs are round or shaped like bird eggs. Some eggs are long and thin, or shaped like balloons. Egg sizes are also different from animal to animal. Some small animals lay lots of tiny eggs, but some larger animals lay fewer, bigger eggs.

## Please Pass the Glue . . .

Insects eggs come in many sizes, shapes, and colors. This shield bug lays oblong-shaped eggs and glues the eggs to leaves with a sticky substance in its saliva.

## Cutworm moth

The eggs of these moths have patterns on the top ends. The eggs are white when they are first laid and turn to dark purple in about a week.

## Octopus

Octopus eggs look like tear-drop shaped balloons. If you look carefully, you can see octopus eyes and tentacles through some of the eggs. These eggs are from Southern Australia.

# Egg Shapes & Sizes

Eggs come in many shapes and sizes. Usually, animals lay a few large eggs or many small eggs. Pointed egg shapes give the embryo more room to grow. Rounder eggs have less surface area so less heat escapes. An egg's shape may also depend on where the eggs are laid. Birds nesting on rocky cliffs usually lay very pointed eggs which cannot roll away too easily.

## Wow, Cool Job!

Scientists measured the heartbeats of emu embryos from outside their eggs.

They found that an emu's heartbeat went down from 175 beats per minute to 145 beats per minute in the days before hatching.

**African ostrich birds** lay the world's largest eggs.

**Chicken eggs** (white and brown)

**Quail bird eggs** (speckled)

**Emu bird egg**

## How small is small?

Hummingbirds are small birds that lay even smaller eggs (left). Cicada bug eggs (on coin) are also tiny, and hundreds of them could fit on a coin. Some female parasites lay millions of eggs at a time. Their eggs are too small to see without a microscope.

**Alligators** Like many reptiles, alligators lay oblong eggs (left). The females lay the eggs in a nest and stay nearby to protect them.

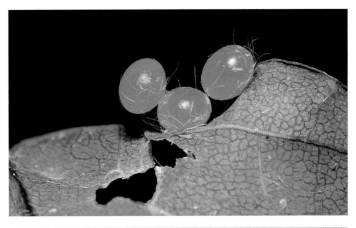

**Oak hawk-moth** Female oak hawk-moths lay their green eggs (above) on the edges of leaves. The caterpillars that hatch from these eggs will also be green, but the adult moths will be brown. The eggs shown here were found in Hungary.

15

# Egg Colors

Many types of animals lay white eggs. Their eggs are white because the outer shells are made from calcium carbonate, like the sidewalk chalk you play with outside. The outer layer of many fish eggs is transparent, which lets us see the fish growing inside the egg (right-hand page, below).

## Where's Dinner? I'm Hungry!

Most snake, lizard, alligator, and crocodile eggs are white. Below, a green python is coming out of its egg. The snake's yellow color will change to green when it gets older.

## Stink bug

This stink bug (left) may have a stinky name, but its small, shiny eggs look like pearls.

## Zooplankton

Some fish eggs (below) float on the water's surface with eggs and larvae from other animals.

# Eggs with a View

# Egg Colors

Give your favorite adult a pop quiz today and ask them what color animal eggs are. You will probably hear a wrong answer. Send him or her back to school! The chicken eggs we eat for breakfast may be white, but eggs from some insects, fish, and birds come in a rainbow of colors.

## Blue, Red, Yellow, Pink, and More!

Biologists do not know why some animals have such brightly colored eggs. Their colors may serve to warn predators that they taste bad. Below, a female shieldbacked pine seed bug has just laid blue eggs!

**Female brown butterflies** (above) lay their round yellow eggs on the undersides of leaves. **Seagrape sawfly** eggs (below) are bright red, just like some parts of their bodies.

Below, a **stink bug** lays pink eggs. There are many species (types) of stink bugs with many different egg colors and shapes.

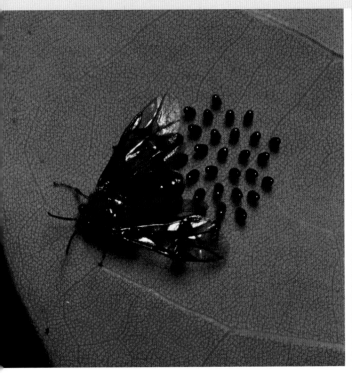

# Egg Colors

Many egg colors are a mystery. Birds that lay eggs in nests in trees often have green or blue eggs, while birds that lay eggs on the ground usually have white eggs. Some biologists believe the bright egg colors remind male birds to help take care of their nests, while other biologists think the green and blue eggs are easier to hide from predators.

## Rule Breakers

Some species (types) of large, ostrich-like birds called emus lay their emerald-green eggs directly on the ground. Their eggs have pointed ends that keep them from rolling away.

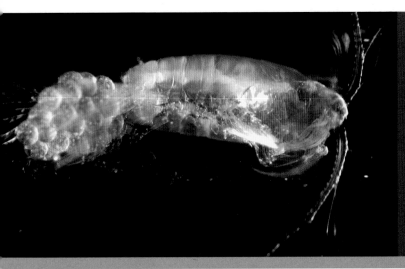

## Copepods

These shrimp-like animals live in fresh and salt water. Their blue eggs hang in grape-like clusters at the backs of their bodies.

## Think Pink!

Apple snails lay their pink eggs in large clusters on plant stems near water. Some apple snails can lay more than 1000 eggs at a time!

# Egg Guarders

Lots of people know birds guard their eggs and their nests, but did you know that some insects and spiders also protect their eggs? Animals that defend their eggs from predators often lay fewer eggs than animals that do not guard their eggs.

## Let's Play Ball!

Or, maybe not. The female black widow spider lays her eggs in a pile and then rolls the eggs up in a ball of silk. She carries the egg sac everywhere, and fights any animal that tries to steal them.

## Spiders
This spider guards her egg sac by wrapping six of her eight legs all the way around it.

## Shield bug
This shield bug from Ecuador and its eggs blend in very well with this tree bark.

# Don't Mess with My Nest!

Many reptiles are "egg dumpers." They lay their eggs in a good place and then leave. Most alligators and crocodiles, though, stay near their nests and attack any animal that comes close to them.

23

# Egg Guarders

Animals guard their eggs for many reasons. Many birds sit on their eggs — called incubation — to keep the embryos inside the eggs from getting too cold or too hot. Some fish stay near their eggs while fanning them with their fins, which moves extra oxygen near the eggs and keeps them clean.

## Don't Look Down!

Storks are large birds and build their nests on top of tall buildings or electricity poles.

## Brrrrrrrrrrr . . .

Penguins lay just one egg. The parents must keep the egg warm under their bodies all of the time, or the growing embryo will die. The male warms the egg while the female hunts for food.

Below, a female angelfish guards her eggs until they hatch. Both the male and the female spend many hours cleaning the leaves before laying and fertilizing their eggs.

## A Clean Start . . .

# Egg Stealers

Eggs are filled with protein and make a high-energy treat for animals searching for food. Some eggs are stolen from hiding places, while other eggs are stolen from nests when Mom or Dad leave to look for their own food. Underwater animals such as catfish also steal eggs.

## Open Wide!

Snakes and lizards can unhinge their jaws so that eggs and other large foods can fit inside their mouths.

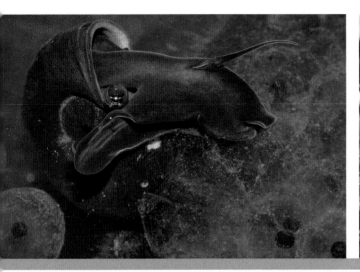

**Snakes and other reptiles** (left and below) are notorious egg thieves. Sometimes they even climb trees to steal eggs from bird nests!

**Snack time!** Above left, a water snail eats unguarded frog eggs in a shallow pond. Above, ants feast on freshly laid fly eggs.

# Puking Eggshells

**A snake has sharp points on the inside of its backbone that crack an egg's shell as it moves through the snake's body. Then the snake spits out the shell.**

# Egg Stealers

Wild animals are not the only egg stealers. Some people steal eggs from bird nests as a hobby or from reptile nests to sell at pet stores. When egg thieves are caught, they can be sent to jail because egg stealing is against the law, especially when the eggs are from rare or endangered animals.

## Have Egg, Will Travel

Rats love chicken eggs, but chicken farmers do not love rats. And here's a mystery: people have found whole eggs in rat nests that are far away from chickens. How do the rats move such large eggs without breaking them?

## Stop, thief!

These thieves have been caught in the act of stealing eggs — a sand goanna from Australia (left), a turkey vulture (below left), and a herring gull (below right) in Sweden with an egg stolen from another bird, a common guillemot.

29

# Egg Shelters

If you know where to look, egg shelters are almost everywhere. Below, female fruit flies are using their ovipositors to place their eggs into an orange. Their ovipositors are long, stick-like parts at the back ends of their bodies that their eggs move through. When the eggs hatch, the larvae will have fresh fruit to eat!

Trick-or-Treat!

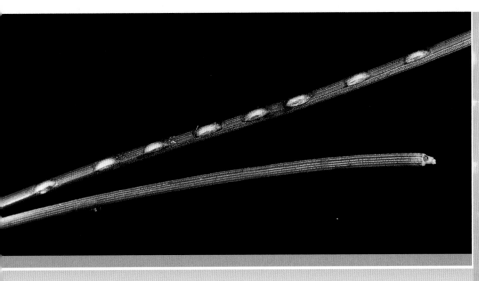

**European pine sawflies** (above) lay their eggs in slits in pine needles, while **squash bugs** (right) lay their eggs on the undersides of leaves.

**Frog eggs** (below) are covered with a "jelly coat" that protects them from damage in water. **Salamander** eggs also have jelly coats.

# Egg Shelters

A good egg detective knows where to to look for animal eggs, even at the beach. Below is a "mermaid's purse," a special casing laid by some sharks and skates, where the eggs will grow. Sometimes the empty egg cases wash up on the shore with seashells. Pieces of turtle egg shells can also be found on beaches.

## Cracking the Case

If you look carefully inside this egg casing, you can see the large yolk sac and a long, slim dogfish shark embryo attached to it.

# Run for Your Life!

Many marine turtles dig holes in beach sand to make their nests. After laying their eggs, the female turtles go back to the ocean.

The hatchlings must climb out of their nest by themselves and get to the ocean before being eaten by predators.

# Egg Shelters

Many types of animals build shelters for their eggs. The type of shelter an animal builds can tell you a lot about where the animal lives and why it needs to protect its eggs. In the nest below, a bird wove feathers into the sticks of the nest to make it warmer. The spots on the eggs help them blend in with the nest so it's harder for egg stealers to see them.

Hide 'n Seek

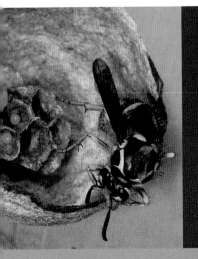

## Home, sweet home

Left, a German yellow jacket builds a nest, then deposits an egg in each cell. The nest is made from chewed wood mixed with saliva.

Below, building a nest on the side of a rocky cliff is hard work. A twig nest would blow off the cliff on a windy day, but these nests made with mud and spit by swallow birds make a safe place to lay eggs.

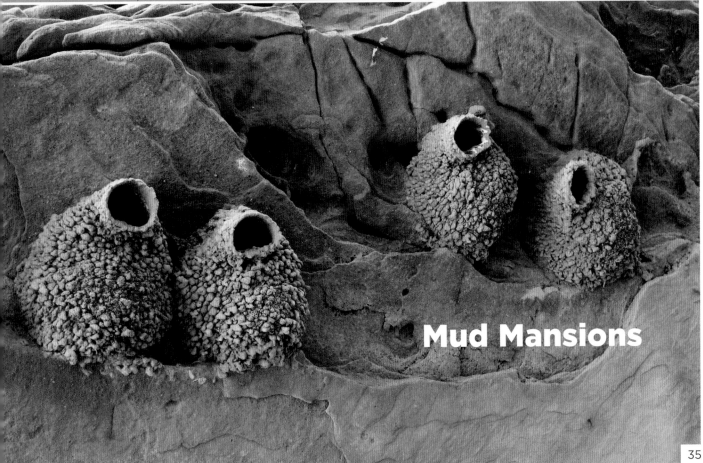

# Mud Mansions

# Egg Escapers

Breaking out of an egg can be hard work for a young animal. Birds and reptiles have a special "egg tooth" that helps them crack open their egg's shell. These animals lose their egg tooth as they grow into adults.

Swan Hatchlings

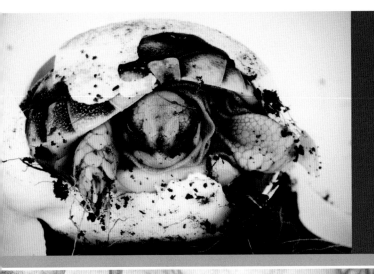

## Turtles

Some turtles stay inside their partially opened shells while they finish absorbing their egg's yellow yolk sac. The yolk sac is high in protein and gives them energy.

## Lizard Hatchlings

# Egg Escapers

Insects do not have egg teeth like snakes, but their fast-growing bodies help them break open their eggs. Some insects, such as the butterfly caterpillars below, eat their way out of their eggshells! Like most newly hatched animals, insects usually look way too big for their eggs.

# Play Time!

**Praying mantis nymphs** emerge from their egg sac. An adult female glued the egg sac to a tree branch, and more than 200 mantid nymphs came out of it.

# Gross or Cool?

The surface of an egg might look plain and boring to your bare eye, but with a very strong microscope, it looks much different. The photos below were made with a scanning electron microscope. They show details of the outside (left) and the inside (right) of a quail bird egg. The openings are large enough to let oxygen gas come inside but not large enough for the embryo or yolk to fall out.

## Python Eggs

After they lay their eggs, female pythons wrap their coils around the eggs to keep them safe and warm. This photo shows the eggs before the female had a chance to lay them.

## Bubble Nests

**Female Siamese fighting fish lay their eggs on the surface of the water and then blow bubbles around the eggs. These bubble nests help keep the eggs safe.**

# Gross or Cool?

Some species (types) of wasps lay their eggs INSIDE butterfly eggs! After the wasp and butterfly eggs hatch, the wasp larvae feed on the caterpillar's flesh. In the picture below, the white, egg-like shapes are cocoons for the wasp's pupae. The pupae will become adult wasps and the caterpillar will die.

Hungry Hitchhikers!

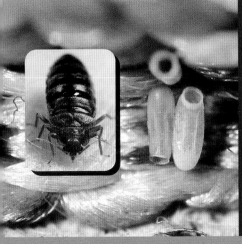

## Don't let the bedbugs bite!

Most people who are bitten by a bedbug never see the bug. The egg casings can be found in infested bed mattresses (left).

## Dad of the year

A male jawfish from the Phillipines keeps his mate's eggs in his mouth for more than a week. This type of egg care is called mouth brooding (below).

## Open Wide!

# Whose Egg Is This?

Now that you have looked at all kinds of eggs from animals around the world, are you a good Egg Detective? Look at the eggs on these two pages and guess what type of animal laid them. **Look on pages 46 and 47 for the answers.**

Take a Wild Guess . . .

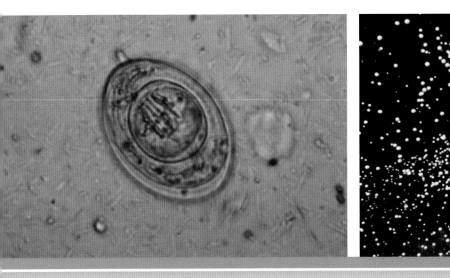

**Whose egg is this?**

**Whose eggs are these?**

Look on page 47 for the answers.

**Whose eggs are these?**

**Whose egg is this?**

Look on page 47 for the answers.

# Whose Egg Is This?

Fossilized dinosaur eggs have been found all over the word.  Some dinosaur eggs are much larger than an ostrich egg, while others are smaller than a turtle egg.   Every once in a while, scientists are lucky enough to find a dinosaur egg with the embryo still inside.  Unfortunately, no one knows what type of dinosaur laid the egg below.

## Fossilized Dinosaur Eggs!

Just like other types of animal eggs, dinosaur eggs come in many shapes and sizes.  You can see dinosaur eggs in museums or at dig sites around the world such as Egg Mountain in Montana in the United States.

At some fossil sites, scientists have found dinosaur egg fossils in places that look like bird nests.  The nests range from simple holes in the ground to nests with their top edges lined in mud.

**Tapeworms**  Tapeworm eggs are released by the millions in the feces (poop) of many mammals.

**Coral**  Coral are small animals that live in large groups under water.  Coral release their eggs at the same time — millions of them!

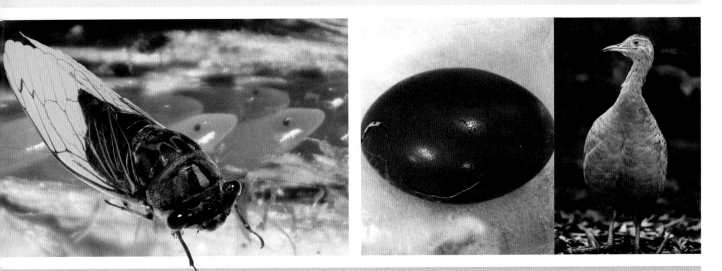

**Cicadas**  The embryos in these cicada eggs are almost finished growing.  The dots on the pointed ends are eyespots.

**Common Tinamou**  This egg was collected in South America by Charles Darwin during his voyage on the HMS Beagle from 1831 to 1836.

## ACKNOWLEDGMENTS

Research from the following biologists and organizations contributed to the information in this book: Jesús M. Avilésae, Linda Fink, A. Ar, E. Gefen, Ivan Gomez-Mestre, Peter Meylan, Anders P. Møllerfg, Juan Morenocd, K. Moriya, J. T. Pearson, Juan J. Solerab, H. Tazawa, Katherine A. Voss-Roberts, Glenn E. Walsberg, Karen Warkentin, Centers for Disease Control, Bugwood, National Oceanic and Atmospheric Administration, and the United States Department of Agriculture.

**Left:** Young wasps growing inside their eggs.

## GLOSSARY

**Brooding**  The act of protecting eggs until they hatch, which can be done by sitting on them in a nest the way birds do or holding them in safe place such as some mouth-brooding fish do.

**Clutch**  A group of eggs laid by birds or reptiles, usually laid at the same time.

**Embryo**  The developing animal in a fertilized egg.

**Hatchlings**  Recently hatched animals.

**Incubating**  The act of keeping eggs warm so the embryos inside can grow; usually done by sitting on the eggs.

**Monotremes**  The two types of mammals that lay eggs, including the duck-billed platypus and the spiny anteater.

**Oology**  The study of eggs.  Many oologists are also egg collectors.

**Pupae**  The name for insects such as flies, butterflies, and moths when they are changing from worm-like bodies stages into their adult bodies.

**Spawning**  The act of releasing eggs in water.  The eggs are called **spawn.**

## INDEX